ACADEMY OF
LEARNING

Your Complete Preschool Lesson Plan Resource: Volume 2

© **2015 Breely, Crush & Associates, LLC**

Ver. 112214

Table of Contents

Educator Biography 3

How to Use This Book 3

Language & Literacy 5

Math & Cognitive 5

Fine Motor Skills...5

Language & Literacy 5

Creative Arts 5

Sensory...5

Dramatic Play & Social Development 5

Science 5

Gross Motor Skills..5

Field Trip Ideas 5

Introduction to the Units 6

Fall..6

Music & Movement 6

Language & Literacy 9

Math & Cognitive 10

Fine Motor Skills...13

Language & Literacy 17

Creative Arts 20

Sensory...20

Dramatic Play & Social Development 21

Science 21

Gross Motor Skills..22

Field Trip Ideas 22

Circus 23

Music & Movement 23

Language & Literacy 25

Math & Cognitive 26

Fine Motor Skills...27

Language & Literacy 30

Creative Arts 30

Sensory...31

Circus (continued)

Dramatic Play & Social Development 31

Science 31

Gross Motor Skills 32

Field Trip Ideas 32

Halloween 33

Music & Movement 33

Language & Literacy 33

Math & Cognitive 34

Fine Motor Skills 38

Language & Literacy 41

Creative Arts 43

Sensory 44

Dramatic Play & Social Development 45

Science 45

Gross Motor Skills 45

Field Trip Ideas 46

Bats & Spiders 47

Music & Movement 47

Language & Literacy 47

Math & Cognitive 48

Fine Motor Skills 49

Language & Literacy 51

Creative Arts 52

Sensory 53

Dramatic Play & Social Development 53

Science 53

Gross Motor Skills 54

Field Trip Ideas 54

Where To Get What You Need 55

Educator Biography

Sharlit Elliott has a B.S. in Elementary Education and Early Childhood from Brigham Young University and has been a teacher for over 15 years working with children ages 3-5. She keeps current on changes in education by attending University classes and conferences several times a year. Besides having raised five children, she has held various leadership positions with the Girl Scouts and the 4-H program. She enjoys gardening, scrapbooking, reading and of course working with children.

How to Use This Book

This book is designed for a teacher working with children ages 3-5 in a classroom, homeschool or home preschool environment. One of the most important aspects of this series is that it includes fun activities that will enhance their skills. These lessons plans, games and ideas are all for you to use. Don't forget, these are complete lessons and activities that have been designed for compliance with federal and state guidelines for education. We go above and beyond to bring you MORE than what's expected in the public school system.

We will refer to your students as "your children or class". That includes whatever area you are using these lessons for: homeschool or preschool. Our lesson plans include improving student's abilities through activities. The skills we will be working with include: listening skills, music, movement, language and literacy, mathematics, science, fine motor, creative art, sensory, dramatic play, and social skills.

The book is organized by themes which will help you quickly find just the right information. The headings in the book will direct you quickly to large group, small group, and free time activities. It will also provide ideas for field trips.

This book will include the following areas:

Group Activities/Circle Time

- Music & Movement is used to help develop large muscles in arms and legs. These need to be developed before children can be successful in small muscles activities such as used in writing or cutting with scissors. This area also helps children learn to enjoy music and the basics such as beat, loud/soft and fast/slow.

- Language & Literacy is how we help children learn vocabulary, story order, thinking skills, recall, concepts of the theme, and expressive language.

Small Group Activities/Table Times

- Math & Cognitive is used to teach numbers, shapes, patterns, sorting, thinking and reasoning skills.

- Fine Motor Skills develop small muscles to be able to draw, write, manipulate small things, to tear, and to cut with scissors.

- Language & Literacy is used to develop skills such as expressive writing, visual memory, matching letters, letter sounds, categorizing items, directional words, and opposites.

- Other creative activities to develop their own uniqueness as an individual.

Free Time

- Creative arts to draw, build, and develop their imagination.

- Sensory activities are used to learn through exploration and using their senses.

- Dramatic Play & Social Development let children take on different roles, solve problems, find solutions, and develop social interactions.

- Science helps children explore by experimenting, identifying problems, guessing what will happen, checking to see what did happen, questioning how things happened, and developing a plan of what to do next.

- Gross Motor Skills to practice using large and small muscles in fun activities.

- Field Trip Ideas to help children use real places to learn about the world.

Throughout the book we will use the following icons to show the different types of activities:

MUSIC & MOVEMENT

LANGUAGE & LITERACY

MATH & COGNITIVE

FINE MOTOR SKILLS

CREATIVE ARTS

SENSORY

DRAMATIC PLAY & SOCIAL DEVELOPMENT

SCIENCE

GROSS MOTOR SKILLS

FIELD TRIP IDEAS

Introduction to the Units

These lesson plans have been used during the fall with great success. Because of different opinions, policies or religions, sometimes Halloween is not observed in a preschool setting. For example, in the federal Head Start programs, holidays are not observed nor are birthdays. With a mixed group of children, all the lesson plans (except Halloween) can be adjusted, modified or used to replace this particular holiday. In this way, children who do observe the holiday at home are still able to enjoy the "season" and other aspects of the holiday in a fun and safe way. Because all these topics take place in the same season, there is a little overlap from unit to unit, allowing you to pick and choose your favorite activities.

Fall

MUSIC AND MOVEMENT

1. Sing the **"Five Little Apples"** to the tune of "Five Monkeys Jumping on the Bed" (Author unknown)

    Way up high in an apple tree,

    Five little apples smiled down at me.

    I shook and shook and shook that tree.

    Four little apples smiled down at me.

    Way up high in an apple tree,

    Four little apples smiled down at me.

    I shook and shook and shook that tree.

    Three little apples smiled down at me.

Way up high in an apple tree,

Three little apples smiled down at me.

I shook and shook and shook that tree.

Two little apples smiled down at me

Way up high in an apple tree,

Two little apples smiled down at me

I shook and shook and shook that tree.

One little apple smiled down at me.

Way up high in an apple tree,

One little apple smiled down at me.

I shook and shook and shook that tree.

No little apples smiled back at me.

2. Sing the song **"Ten Little Leaves"**

This song variation can be used when children have master counting to five.

Use the same words in Five Little Apples, but replace apples with the word leaves.

Also use numbers 10 instead of five. Continue counting backwards in song until you reach no little leaves smiled back at me.

Example:

Way up high in an old oak tree,

Ten little leaves smiled down at me.

I shook and shook and shook that tree.

Nine little leaves smiled down at me.

3. Sing **"One Little Apple"**

> One little apple
>
> Round and red
>
> Fell cur-plunk on (name of child's) head.

Use an apple to softly touch each child's head when you say their name. Continue singing song until each child has been named. This song can be used to help children learn each other's names and you give a dismissal to leave the circle.

4. The following are a list of additional songs that you can play and sing for the fall unit:

> "Hear the Wind Blow" found in *I Have A Song For You – Volume 1* by Janeen Brady.
>
> "Mister Wind is a Mischief" found in *I Have A Song For You – Volume 1* by Janeen Brady.
>
> "It's Autumn Time" found in *The Children's Songbook* of The Church of Jesus Christ of Latter-Day Saints.
>
> "The Leaves of the Trees" by Irmgard Fuertges found in *More Piggy Back Songs* compiled by Jean Warren.
>
> "Fall Leaves" by Pamela Moyer found on tape from Macmillan Sign & Learn.
>
> "Nutty Squirrel" by Pamela Moyer found on tape from Macmillan Sign & Learn.
>
> "One Little, Two Little, Three Little Pumpkins" found in *Piggy Back Songs* compiled by Jean Warren.
>
> "Wiggle Wobble" found on CD We All Live Together Volume 1 by Greg & Steve

These songs can all be found on CDs available on Half.com or Amazon.com, sometimes in good but used condition for a significant discount.

LANGUAGE AND LITERACY

These are some books that are great to read to the children:

> Clifford Loves Autumn by Norman Bridwall

> Leaf Seasons by Quinlan B. Lee

> Possum's Harvest Moon by Anne Hunter

> When Autumn Comes by Robert Maass

> Red Leaf, Yellow Leaf by Lois Ehlert

> Fresh Fall Leaves by Betsy Franco

> Fall Changes by Ellen B. Senisi

> It's Pumpkin Time! By Zoe Hall

> Who's got the Apple? By Jan Loof

> The Apple Pie Tree by Zoe Hall

> Pumpkin Pumpkin by Jeane Titherington

Read a new book each day and ask questions about the pictures in the book, (What colors do you see? What happened to the fresh leaves?) After reading each book ask the children questions about what they enjoyed about the book, such as "What was your favorite part of what happens when autumn came?" Then follow it up by asking what their family does in the fall or autumn. Be sure and let them know fall and autumn mean the same thing.

Another activity that increases their language skills would be to read Red Leaf, Yellow Leaf and to discuss with the children the different colors and sizes of leaves. Next tell the children that they will be going outside to collect leaves. The children will collect a few leaves each that they like and bring them into class when teacher gives the signal. Children will come to the circle and take turns showing their leaves. Later in small groups have each child describe their leaves, such as a tiny, yellow leaf with brown spots. The children will glue them on a piece of paper and the teacher will write next to each leaf, the child's description. Hang the pictures around the room.

Be sure and read The Apple Pie Tree or another book that tells how apples grow. Talk about the sequence of events that produce apples. Also, when reading it have the children notice the bird's nest and what is happening there, this helps them see that the events of growing apples and birds takes time to grow and develop. Next have them tell you their favorite parts of the story, so that they can express their own thoughts and by doing so helping them remember what they learned.

SMALL GROUP ACTIVITIES/TABLE TIMES

MATH & COGNITIVE

When cooking with the children do the activity at the very start of their class so you have time to complete activity and have time for them sample the food.

Apple Dessert

Make apple dessert with the children. Use plastic knives that have a cutting edge. Be sure and talk with them about keeping their hands clean hands while cooking. Prepare a poster board before you start with pictures of the ingredients in the recipe that you will use to make the apple dessert. Example: one apple, draw a tsp. showing sugar and so on.

Purchase these items ahead of time: one apple for each child to prepare, 1 tsp. sugar for per apple used, 1/4 Tsp cinnamon per apple and 1 Tb. of raisins per apple.

Make sure that you have measuring spoons ready. First, have children wash their hands and then second, have them wash the apples. If you have an apple peeler/corer use it to prepare the apples by letting them take turns turning the handle. If not, use a corer/slicer that you push the apple through. Then peel or cut off peelings and children will cut their apple into small pieces with a plastic serrated knife. Next have the children follow the recipe pictures in adding all the ingredients to a pan big enough to cook that many apples in.

Talk about the pictures and the numbers while adding the amounts. Add 1 or 2 Tbs. per apple and cook on low or use a crock pot to cook. The time needed to cook them will depend on the amount of apples and the size of the apples, so do this project early so the children can smell it cooking and still have time to eat it.

You can save the seeds from the apples to count on another day. Also, on another day they can draw different colors of apples and glue the seeds in center of apple pictures while counting how many seeds they used in each apple.

Roasted Pumpkin Seeds

Another cooking activity is roasting pumpkin seeds. Purchase small pumpkins for each child, or use a few large pumpkins to share. Prepare a poster for the recipe by using pictures like the Apple Dessert recipe.

Have children wash the pumpkins. Use volunteers or you can cut off the lid of each pumpkin. Next have the children discover what is inside by pulling and scraping. Have them save their pumpkin seeds in a bowl.

Now take turns counting some of the seeds in the bowl. Next follow the poster directions which are to combine 1 cup unwashed seeds, 1/4 tsp. Worcestershire sauce, 1 Tbs. butter or margarine, 3/4 tsp. salt.

*These ingredients can be doubled if you have lots of seeds.

Spread seed mixture into a shallow baking pan and bake for two hours at 250 degrees. Stir occasionally until seeds are crisp, dry and golden. When the seeds are cool, eat them shell and all.

Leaf Order Size

Collect leaves with the children outside or bring some to school. Have paper and glue ready for this project. Children pick a large leaf to glue on the left size of their paper. Next have them find a very small leaf to glue on the right side of their paper. Then have them find a middle size leaf to put in the center of the page. If they can put the leaves in order with only three sizes, make it harder by using four leaves in order size.

Apple Number Game

For this game, prepare a simple tree using brown paper. Then glue the tree cut out shape on a blue paper background. Next laminate the square. Prepare small apples from red paper and laminate them. Public schools usually have small die cuts for apples and will often let you use them, if it's for a school.

Make a spinner for the game by making a small circle and cutting it out. Put even lines across the circle and write numbers 1-5 or 1-10 in each section. You can add dots to each section in place of the numbers or use both dots and numbers. Punch a hole in the center by using a nail. Make a small spinner hand with a hole in it. Then, laminate all the pieces. Cut the pieces apart and place a brad through the hand and through the circle. This will be the spinner for the game.

To play the game, place the tree game board and the apple pieces on the table. Children will take turns spinning the spinner, saying the number and/or counting the dots. Then they will add that amount of apples to the tree. Continue the game until the apples are all gone or the children lose interest.

This activity will help them recognize numerals and learn how many things the numeral represents. It also reinforces counting skills.

Pumpkin Game

Teacher makes small pumpkins or uses a die cut machine. Write on the pumpkins with dots on each card representing numerals 1-10 and a second set with numbers 1-10.

Game 1
Children can take turns naming the numerals by counting the dots on the pumpkins.

Game 2
Children can match the numerals on the pumpkins to the correct number card using the dots on the cards.

Soft Play Dough

2 cups flour
1 cup salt
2 cups water
2 Tbs. cream of tartar
2 Tbs. cooking oil

*Food coloring optional

Combine all ingredients in a medium sauce pan, mix well. Cook over low heat stirring constantly until mixture gathers and forms a dough. Dump onto counter until cool enough to handle and then knead to form a ball. Store in a container or plastic bag.

*Food coloring may be added to the water before mixing with the flour.

Play-dough Counting

Another activity for counting can be done by using play-dough. You can use cookie cutter shapes; ghosts, pumpkins, witches, leaves, headstones etc. Use small rolling pins to cut out and line up the shapes and count them. On another day you can make a pattern with the play-dough. Start with two patterns and add up to four to expand their thinking skills when they can do smaller numbers of patters. This activity helps them see patterns in numerals and other things around them. This increases their problem solving skills.

FINE MOTOR SKILLS

Apple Prints

Cut apples in half and show the children the star inside the apple created by the seeds.

In advance, prepare paint colors yellow-green, yellow, green, and red paint mixed with dish soap. Put the paint on foam trays from the bakery. Show the children different colors and types of apples, which should match the paint colors. Cut the apples in half with seeds showing. It is important to cut the apples as smoothly and flat as possible so that they will make good prints of the seeds inside. Next, let the children dip cut side of apple into the paint and use as a stamp. Use one hand to hold down the paper while pulling up the apple. Continue printing/stamping the apples until they are happy with how it looks. This develops hand-eye coordination.

Fall Tree

Prepare a brown construction paper tree trunk and small squares of yellow, red, orange, and brown crepe-paper. Create one tree trunk for each child.

Pattern below:

Children glue the trunk onto their paper in the position they desire. Next they hold a pencil and place a piece of the crepe-paper over the eraser end and hold it tightly around the pencil. Then they dip the end into a small puddle of glue and then press it on to the paper around the tree trunk to make leaves. Children keep adding leaves until they are happy with how it looks. This help to develop eye-hand coordination.

If you want to do this as a two day project, you would make poster board trunk patterns for children to trace around with a pencil on brown construction paper. Then they would cut on the lines they traced to make their own tree trunk. The next day they could make the leaves for it. This activity improves their writing and cutting skills.

Another variation of this project would be to have them both trace and cut the trunk and glue on the page, but use small sponges to dip into leaf colors and print them around the trunk to create leaves.

Stencil Tracers

Use stencils of fall objects or make your own fall shape with poster board and have children trace around them using colored pencils on a piece of while paper. Example of shapes you could make are: pumpkins, bats, ghosts. This activity helps develop writing skills.

Play Dough Pumpkins

Make soft orange play dough and have children make pumpkins of different sizes and shapes. You can also use the self hardening type of dough. If using the self-hardening type you can leave it white or color it. Then when it dries out, the children can paint it with water colors or poster paint. This activity develops finger strength.

Self-Hardening Play Dough

4 cups flour
11/2 cups salt
1 tsp. alum

*Optional 1-2 Tbs. food coloring

Mix the flour, salt and alum together. Then add the water to it gradually.

* If you want mixture colored, add coloring to water before before stirring into the flour for a smooth color.

Stir to form a ball in bowl. Add more water if it won't hold together, Next knead dough. Place in a sealed container until ready to use. After shapes have been made leave out to dry.

Leaf Rubbing

Teacher or children collect different sizes of leaves. Teacher puts masking tape on the smooth side of the leaf. Then tape the leaf to the table with the leaf veins or bumpy side up and the smooth side down. Demonstrate to the children how to place the white paper over the leaf. Next, show how to use an unwrapped crayon on the paper. Rub the crayon back and forth across the paper while holding the crayon in a horizontal or flat position while using downward pressure. The leaf's shape and veins will appear. This activity develops finger strength and eye-hand coordination.

Leaf Printing

First, collect different sizes of leaves. Make sure the children are wearing painting aprons. Then the children will choose a leaf and paint one side of it. Then they place the leaf onto a piece of paper with the paint side down on the page and smooth it down carefully. This will create a leaf print. They can continue with this project using different sizes of leaves and different paint colors.

Paper Tearing Project

Draw a large pumpkin on a piece of white card-stock or construction paper. Children cut out the pumpkins. Then demonstrate how to tear colored paper into small pieces and glue them onto the pumpkin shape. They can use orange, yellow and green paper to create their pumpkin with a stem or they can make it into a jack-o-lantern with eyes, mouth and nose.

Mr. Potato Pumpkin

Take the pieces from a Mr. Potato Head toy and let the children put a face on the pumpkin. You may want to place holes in the pumpkin before hand to make it easier. Let the children play with re-arranging the pumpkin.

Simple Pumpkin

For a simple pumpkin use white paper plates and have children paint them with orange paint. Then have children glue on a simple green stem. When they are day hang them around the classroom.

Or you can have children make them into jack-o-lanterns. Provide yellow construction paper squares, triangles and two different mount shapes. Children will choose shapes of eyes, nose and mouth and glue them onto their pumpkins.

More Simple Projects

Teacher will show children how to draw several fall shapes such as leaves, apples, pumpkins, etc., using colored chalk. Next children will be given black construction paper and told to use the colored chalk to create their own fall pictures.

Owl

Use an empty toilet paper roll for owl body. Squeeze top of roll together and staple it closed. Make brown paint or use tole paint and have children paint it brown. Use cardstock or poster board to make two small wings.

Cut wings out. Children will paint them with the body. When body and wings are dry, children will glue the wings on the owl body. They will also glue on two wiggly craft eyes and an orange beak made by you. To make beak use a small rectangle piece of orange construction paper. Fold it over and cut a narrow triangle shape with the wide base part forming the part they will attach to the owl for its beak.

LANGUAGE AND LITERACY

Apple Game

Make 24 apples using paper colored yellow, red and green. Then make two sets of identical apple faces. Make each set different from the other sets by changing the eyes and or mouths and colors of the sets. Mount three different apples on a narrow piece of poster board and matching ones on squares. Proceed until the narrow cards and made and matching ones are mounted on individual squares. Then laminate them so that you can use them many times. See example below.

Use this game to teach visual discrimination, vocabulary and colors names.

Instructions – give each child a long narrow card and put square matching cards in the middle of the table face down in a stack. Tell the children that they will take turns drawing a card from the pile in the middle of the table and see if it will match any of the apples on their card. If it matches a card they will put it on top of that card. They will also tell what color the apple is and if the mouth looks happy, sad or surprised or etc. They will also tell how the eyes are – both open, closed etc. If the card did not match their card the child will leave the card face up in the middle of the table. The next player can take the apple card that is face up or draw from the pile. Play continues until all the players have matching apples on them. Use this game more than once during the week. Children like repetition but not everyday.

Pumpkin Game

Purchase small plastic pumpkins at a party store or dollar store that are open at the top and also small votive candles. You will need one set for each member of the small group and one for the teacher to demonstrate with. If not available, use paper pumpkin shapes and birthday candles in place of the plastic pumpkins.

Use this game to teach position words – in, on, out, over, under, beside, in front of, and behind.

Instructions – Teacher will say one of the position words (like on the pumpkin) and place her candle on the pumpkin. Teacher will tell children to also place their candle on the pumpkin. Children will continue to place their candle in, behind or etc as teacher says the words and demonstrates. Teacher will take notice of the words children understand and which ones they need help doing. Continue play using most familiar word positions like in and on and adding less familiar ones as the children learn them. Use this activity more than one day, keeping it for short periods of time. When the children are beginning to understand where to put candles and the words used, have them take turns telling the other children where to put their candle and demonstrating where to put it.

Leaf Games

Use leaf punch outs from a school supply store or use leaf stickers and place them on squares of poster board. Make a set of four from each sticker design or leaf color. Each child will need four sets of four. Example red leaves, four brown leaves, four yellow leaves and four orange leaves.

1st Game
Give each child at the small group table a set of leaf squares in different colors or designs and have the child make a two color or design pattern with you helping them. Next have them copy your pattern right below. Continue using a two pattern (two different kinds of leaf squares) until they understand it. Make increases in the pattern from two to three kinds and then to a four pattern as children learn over time. You can use these pattern cards over the year so they can make patterns on their own.

2nd Game
Give each child a four color set of cards that have been mixed up and have children sort the cards into the four different colors or designs. Have the child tell you how the cards are different or the same.

<u>3rd Game</u>

Use one set of cards for two children or two sets of cards for four children. Teacher places the cards with the design or color face down on the table. Children will be playing a concentration game. Children will take turns turning three cards over one at a time to find two cards that match. If the child matches two cards, the child tells the color of the leaves that matched and keeps it in front of her/him. Next the child turns the third card face down and places it where the card was before. If the child does not make a match, the child tells the color of each leaf and turns each card facedown while placing it where it was before. The next child to the left takes a turn. The play continues until all the cards have been used up. At the end tell the children that they all did a good job of following directions. They may count all of their cards together with help.

Finger Play Activity

Use a simple finger play such as <u>Five Little Pumpkins</u>. Repeat the words while pointing to your fingers. You can also use pumpkin stickers on a ring of card stock for each finger to act it out or just put a sticker on each of the five fingers.

This activity will help children to increase their memory and learn sequence order.

Five Little Pumpkins

Five little pumpkins sitting on a gate,

The first one said, "Oh my, it's getting late." (point to 1st finger)

The second one said, "There are witches in the air".

The third one said, "But we don't care."

The fourth one said, "Let's run and run and run".

The fifth one said, "I'm ready for some fun."

"Oo-oo!" went the wind and out went the light, (clap hands)

And the five little pumpkins rolled out of sight. (roll hands)

FREE TIME

CREATIVE ARTS

Cut out large fall shapes for the children to paint on. Clip the shapes to the easels. You can also have children cut out the fall shapes days before using the paint or on the same day that the paint is out. Mix orange, red, yellow and green poster paints in containers to be used with paint brushes or use sponge painting on the shapes.

Children will dip the sponge into the paint and then press it on to the shape. To make the sponges cut regular household sponges into squares, triangles, and circles. Next mount the sponges onto blocks of wood or empty spools of thread by gluing them onto the top or bottom. This will help the children keep their fingers clean while painting.

Use shallow containers in the tray with poster paint left thick and only a half of inch or so deep. Don't forget to mix the paint with a little dish detergent to help the paint come out of children's clothes easier.

Other fall shapes can be used on the easel for different days such as large leaf shapes and different squash shapes.

SENSORY

Place a large pumpkin, apples or squash inside the table. Have the pumpkin, apples or squash cut open so children can explore the insides using spoons.

Use a collection of fall leaves mixed with pinecones to explore. Add hidden small shapes later for the children to find.

Make green goblin goop and children to play in and see how a sold changes to a liquid in their hands.

Green Goblin Goop

Use 1 part water to 2 parts corn starch and add enough green washable poster paint to make color desired. Mix together the liquids with the corn starch. The mixture will look like a solid, but when you take a handful, it will become runny and drip out of your hand. If the mixture is too runny and will not form a solid ball add more corn starch. If the mixture is too hard, add a little more water.

DRAMATIC PLAY & SOCIAL DEVELOPMENT

Have a box of costumes or community helper clothing for children to wear. Examples of community helpers are policemen, firemen, nurses, doctors, dentists, etc. You could also use a box of old Halloween costumes. A good place to find these items would be at a local Thrift Store. Your dress up clothes inventory can grow over time, especially if you send a note to parents to see if they have old costumes to donate.

SCIENCE

Display different squash plants and have them cut open so children can compare the insides and seed sizes. Have magnifying glasses available.

Have real or man-made fall leaves for the children to examine. Also include different pine cones and nuts in their shells. Children can compare sizes and colors. If no one is allergic to nuts you could also have some for them to sample.

GROSS MOTOR SKILLS

Apple Toss

Pitch bean bags (apples) into holes of a tree. Make it by using a poster board and attaching it to the front of a large open box.

Leaf Hop

Place pictures of leaves on the floor in a circle or other shape. Children will hop from one sheet to another when music starts or teacher says go and stop when music stops and she says freeze. Teacher will tell them different movement the next time like tip toe and stomp. Continue for 2 or 3 times and then stop until another day. If you stop playing before they are tired of it they will want to play again another day.

FIELD TRIP IDEAS

Fall Walk

Teacher has children looking for signs of fall or autumn outdoors on a short walking field trip or arrange for transportation to a park for this walking field trip. Children tell teacher when they see fall signs. Give each child a bag or grocery sack. Then children are instructed to collect leaves, pine cones and dried small plants. When they have collected enough, bring them into the classroom circle and discuss what they found. Then at table time have them glue their objects to a large piece of paper and write what the children say about the objects that they found.

Another activity you can do after the fall walk is to have the children find leaves that they find interesting. When you get back to class, have the children lay the leaves flat on construction paper. They can do a crayon rubbing to just design the part of the paper that is not covered. Once they are done drawing, cover the front and back with contact paper. You have now made placemats for them to use in school or take home.

Circus

🎵 MUSIC AND MOVEMENT

Play the music from the movie <u>Dumbo</u> by Walt Disney.

1. Sing **Let's Go to the Circus** (Sung To: "Mary Had a Little Lamb")

    Let's go to the Circus

    Let's all go to the circus

    The circus today, the circus today

    Let's all go to the circus, today

    And watch a big parade

    See the clowns all tumbling around, tumbling around

    See the clowns all tumbling around

    In the circus ring.

    Lions and tigers jumping through hoops

    Jumping through hoops, jumping through hoops

    Lions and tigers jumping through hoops

    In their circus cage

    The prancing horses step so high, Step so high, step so high.

    The prancing horses step so high

    In the circus ring

2. Sing **"Take Me Out to the Circus"** sung to the tune of "Take Me Out to the Ball Game"

> Take me out to the circus
>
> Take me to the big top
>
> I want to see the clowns tumbling fast
>
> As I eat popcorn and drink soda pop
>
> Oh, the lions and tigers they may scare me
>
> And the high wire acts amaze
>
> So . . .You! . . .see . . .all the great things we will do
>
> On our circus day

3. Sing **"I'm Walking to the Circus"** sung to the tune of "I've Been Working on the Railroad"

> I am walking through the circus (walk in place)
>
> Happy as can be (make a big smile)
>
> I am walking through the circus (walk in place)
>
> Just to see, what I can see (make binoculars with you hands)
>
> I can see a clown laughing (ha, ha, ha)
>
> I can see an elephant, too (make trunk motion)
>
> I can see a lion sleeping (yawn)
>
> Look out (make binoculars with hands)... because he sees you too!

LANGUAGE AND LITERACY

These are some books that are great to read to the children:

All Aboard the Circus Train by Laura Driscoll

Circus by Lois Ehlert

Bears on Wheels by Jan and Stan Berenstain

Clifford at the Circus by Norman Bridwell

Dumbo by Walt Disney

Circus Finger Play

This little clown is fat and gray (hold up thumb)

This little clown does tricks all day (hold up next finger)

This little clown is tall and strong (hold up next finger)

This little clown is wee and small (hold up next finger)

And this little clown can do anything at all (hold up little finger)

www.academyoflearningonline.com

SMALL GROUP ACTIVITIES/TABLE TIMES

MATH & COGNITIVE

Soft Play Dough

2 cups flour
1 cup salt
2 cups water
2 Tbs. cream of tartar
2 Tbs. cooking oil

*Food coloring optional

Combine all ingredients in a medium sauce pan, mix well. Cook over low heat stirring constantly until mixture gathers and forms a dough. Dump onto counter until cool enough to handle and then knead to form a ball. Store in a container or plastic bag.

*Food coloring may be added to the water before mixing with the flour.

Play-dough counting

Another activity for counting is cookie cutter shapes; clowns, balls, lions, etc and small rolling pins so cut out and line up the shapes and count them. They could also make a pattern with them another day. Start with two patterns and add up to four to expand their thinking skills when they can do smaller numbers of patters. This activity helps them see patterns in numerals and other things around them. This teaches them to solve problems.

Cookie Cutter Fun

Use cookie cutters to make shapes to make a carousel with horses and other animals. You can use the play-dough, cookie dough, bread or other treats.

Clown Hat

Before class, you will need to cut out hat patterns from large pieces of paper. You can get butcher paper from office supply stores or school supply stores in many different colors. Example below:

Children use colored bingo markers to decorate hat with dots. You can also use the Crayola Stamps Markers. Next they count the dots with the teacher. Teacher or child with help writes the numeral. The hat is taped together when dry as part of the clown costume.

✂ FINE MOTOR SKILLS

Clown Collar

Teacher cuts out collar pattern from paper roll. Pattern below:

Teacher uses sponge shapes or makes shapes by cutting them from potatoes with a knife. Teacher prepares poster paint by mixing in a tablespoon of dish soap into each color of paint to help if it gets on clothing.

Put the paint on small foam trays from bakery department. Children will dip sponge or potatoes shapes in to paint and then on the collar paper to decorate it. Next they will tell you the names of the shapes they used. Example heart, star, square. When it is dry, tape around the child's neck for clown costume or save for the day you do your actual circus.

Play Dough Shapes

Make soft play dough and have children make balls of different sizes and shapes or have them create acrobats or their own acts from the circus. You can also use the self-hardening type. If using the self-hardening type you can leave it white or color it. Then when it dries out children can paint it with water colors or poster paint. This activity develops finger strength.

Self-Hardening Play Dough

4 cups flour	Mix the flour, salt and alum together. Then add the water to it gradually.
11/2 cups salt	
1 tsp. alum	* If you want mixture colored, add coloring to water before stirring into the flour for a smooth color.
*Optional 1-2 Tbs. food coloring	
	Stir to form a ball in bowl. Add more water if it won't hold together. Next, knead dough. Place in a sealed container until ready to use. After shapes have been made leave out to dry.

Paper Tearing Project

Teacher draws large clown face on a piece of white card-stock or construction paper. Children cut around the outline. Then teacher demonstrates how to tear colored paper into small pieces and glue them onto the shape. They can use different colored paper to create a clown face of their choosing. Other circus shapes can also be substituted such as a circus tent, circus animals, circus train, etc.

More Simple Projects

Teacher will show children how to draw several simple circus shapes such as a clown, lion, elephants, circus tent, circus train, etc., using colored chalk. Next children will be given black construction paper and told to use the colored chalk to create their own circus pictures.

Face Paint for Clown Costume

Place long mirrors on table top by laying them on their side and using strapping tape to attach them to the table. Have small amounts of water in bowls with colored chalk. Children will dip colored chalk into water and paint with it on their own faces. Examples would be circles on cheeks, heart on forehead etc. Colored chalk usually washes off easily. Try yours out before time to see how your brand works.

Elephant Ears

Use paper-cutter (it works easier to make long perfect strips) to cut long two inch wide head band for ears from gray construction paper. Trace large ears on long size construction paper that has been folded to form normal size or use two regular pieces that have been stapled together on all sides. Make tracer patterns from poster board. Children will trace one large ear on folded or staples paper and trace ear pattern. Next they will cut it out on the lines. Teacher will staple ears to the head band. Child can now wear the ears to be an elephant.

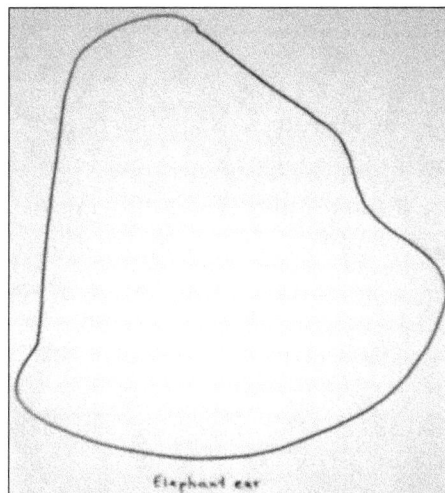

Elephant ear

LANGUAGE AND LITERACY

Sing **"Did You Ever See a Clown?"** Sung to the tune of "Did You Ever See A Lassie?"

Did you ever see a clown,

A clown, a clown?

Did you ever see a clown

Move this way and that?

Move this way and that way,

Move this way and that way.

Did you ever see a clown

Move this way and that?

CREATIVE ARTS

Pretend Activity

Use costumes for this activity. The costumes could be community helper or circus related. Children in a small group will take turns choosing a costume to put on. Next teacher will ask the children if the costumed child is a real (example-clown) or just pretending by wearing a clown costume. We will go through this activity until all the children in the small group have had a turn putting on a costume. Next we will discuss more about what is real and what is pretend.

This activity helps children to use expressive language and helps them learn the difference between real and pretend.

Circus Game

Choose four small circus objects found at The Dollar Tree or Partyland, such as small plastic animals. Use a piece of cloth or a hand towel. Show the items to the children. Say the names of each item while pointing to them. Tell the children that you are going to cover the items up and change their order. Children should study their order before the teacher covers them up.

Next cover the items and change their positions. Uncover the items and start with the child to your left and have he/she put the items back in the order shown. If the children have a hard find doing this use only three items under they get better at doing it. Keep going to the left until all the children in the small group have had at least three turns. If they aren't tired of the game, have them take turns doing the teacher part. They move the items while they are covered and the other children put them back. When they are staring to get restless stop and continue another day. This activity helps children learn develop their visual memory.

SENSORY

Put sand into the sensory table. Then add zoo animals to the sand which you can find at school supply stores or in the toy department at stores like Wal-Mart or Target. Then add plastic berry baskets (like the ones that raspberries and strawberries come in) for cages. Go ahead and also add toy people and if possible circus props. Children will enjoy having their own miniature circus.

DRAMATIC PLAY & SOCIAL DEVELOPMENT

Have a box of costumes or community helper clothing for children to wear. You could also use a box of circus costumes, clowns, Indians, cowboys, etc. A good place to find these items would be at a local Thrift Store.

SCIENCE

Purchase balloons or party favors that expand or shoot out when air is blown into them. You can also talk about different types of gasses. Blow up one balloon with air and one with helium. Show the children the difference between the two. Many Target and Kmart stores offer helium balloon tanks for purchase for about $20-30 which will fill many balloons, much more than just for this project.

Popcorn can be another interesting project for this unit. Popcorn is a great healthy treat and children can watch the kernels turn inside out with an air pop corn popper. Let the children handle the kernels and watch the entire process.

GROSS MOTOR SKILLS

Use a small balance beam that lays flat on the floor. To modify you can use a 2 by 4 or just create a line with colored painter (masking) tape. Painters tape is blue and can be found at Home Depot, Lowe's or similar store. Have the children take turns walking on the "balance beam" jumping through "flames of fire" (hula hoops) and doing summer salts. Let the children practice and have fun.

FIELD TRIP IDEAS

The best field trip idea for this unit is to visit an actual circus. However, based on the schedule for many of these traveling shows, this may not be practical. Instead, you may be able to have one come to you. Many clowns, mimes, and other performers are willing to do visits to your classroom, many without cost. Check with your local government programs as these visits can sometimes to tied to other government programs allowing you to use the resources for free. If you have no other alternatives, check with parents to see if they would be willing to attend as a clown, juggler, etc. Or you can have the children put on a program for parents with their own "tricks" such as the balance beam, cartwheels, juggling, limbo under a stick, hula hoping, jump roping, etc.

Halloween

🎵 MUSIC AND MOVEMENT

The following are great songs to sing for Halloween:

"Ten Little Witches" found in *Wee Sing* by Pamela Conn Beall and Susan Hagen Nipp.

"Spooky Walk" by John Given found in Macmillan *Sing and Learn*.

"The Scary Song" by David Rollins found in Macmillan *Sing and Learn*.

"The Magic Shoes" by Dennis Scott found in Macmillan *Sing and Learn*.

"One Little, Two Little, Three Little Pumpkins" Songs found in *Piggy Back* by Jean Warren.

"The Goblin in the Dark" found in *Piggy Back* by Jean Warren.

"Jack-O-Lantern" found in *Piggy Back* by Jean Warren.

"Witches' Brew" found on tape *Witches' Brew* by Hap Palmer.

"Looking for Dracula" found on CD *10 Carrot Diamond* by Charlotte Diamond.

"Those Bones" found on CD *Five Little Monkeys* by Kimbo Educational.

🔤 LANGUAGE AND LITERACY

There any many great books that you can read to the class for Halloween. Here are some favorites that classes really enjoy:

It's Pumpkin Time! by Zoe Hall

Curious George's Halloween by Robert Bright

Franklin's Halloween by Paulette Bourgeois, Brenda Clark

Froggy's Halloween by Jonathan London

Green Wilma by Tedd Arnold

The Halloween Play by Felicia Bond

My Working Mom by Peter Glassman

Ten Timid Ghosts by Jennifer O'Connell

The Dark at the Top of the Stairs by Sam McBratney

Clifford's First Halloween by Norman Brinswell

The Hurry Up Halloween Costume by Sarah Albee

The Run Away Pumpkin by Kevin Lewis

Woo! The Not So Scary Ghost by Ana Martin Larranaga

SMALL GROUP ACTIVITIES/TABLE TIMES

MATH & COGNITIVE

When cooking with the children do the activity at the very start of their class so you have time to complete activity and have time for them sample the food.

Apple Dessert

Make apple dessert with the children. Use plastic knives that have a cutting edge. Be sure and talk with them about keeping their hands clean hands while cooking. Prepare a poster board before you start with pictures of the ingredients in the recipe that you will use to make the apple dessert. Example: one apple, draw a tsp. showing sugar and so on.

Purchase these items ahead of time: one apple for each child to prepare, 1tsp. sugar for per apple used, 1/4 tsp. cinnamon per apple and 1 Tb. of raisins per apple.

Make sure that you have measuring spoons ready. First, have children wash their hands and then second, have them wash the apples. If you have an apple peeler/corer use it to prepare the apples by letting them turn the handle. If not, use a corer/slicer that you push the apple through. Then peel or cut off peelings and children will cut their apple into small pieces with a plastic serrated knife. Next have the children follow the recipe pictures in adding all the ingredients to a pan big enough to cook that many apples in.

Talk about the pictures and the numbers while adding the amounts. Add 1 or 2 Tbs. per apple and cook on low or use a crock pot to cook. The time needed to cook them will depend on the amount of apples and the size of the apples, so do this project early so the children can smell it cooking and this have time to eat it.

You can save the seeds from the apples to count on another day. Also, on another day they can draw different colors of apples and glue the seeds in center of apple pictures while counting how many seeds they used in each apple.

Roasted Pumpkin Seeds

Another cooking activity is roasting pumpkin seeds. Purchase small pumpkins for each child, or use a few large pumpkins to share. Prepare a poster for the recipe by using pictures like the Apple Dessert recipe.

Have children wash the pumpkins. Use volunteers or you can cut off the lid of each pumpkin. Next have the children discover what is inside by pulling and scraping. Have them save their pumpkin seeds in a bowl.

Now take turns counting some of the seeds in the bowl. Next follow the poster directions which are to combine 1 cup unwashed seeds, 1/4 tsp. Worcestershire sauce, 1 Tbs. butter or margarine, 3/4 tsp. salt.

*These ingredients can be doubled if you have lots of seeds.

Spread seed mixture into a shallow baking pan and bake for two hours at 250 degrees. Stir occasionally until seeds are crisp, dry and golden. When the seeds are cool eat them shell and all.

Leaf Order Size

Collect leaves with the children outside or bring some to school. Have paper and glue ready for this project. Children pick a large leaf to glue on the left size of their paper. Next have them find a very small leaf to glue on the right side of their paper. Then have them find a middle size leaf to put in the center of the page. If they can put the leaves in order with only three sizes, make it harder by using four leaves in order size.

Apple Number Game

For this game, prepare a simple tree using brown paper. Then glue the tree cut out shape on a blue paper background. Next laminate the square. Prepare small apples from red paper and laminate them. Public schools usually have small die cuts for apples and will often let you use them, if it's for a school. Make a spinner for the game by making a small circle and cutting it out. Put even lines across the circle and write numbers 1-5 or 1-10 in each section. You can add dots to each section in place of the numbers or use both dots and numbers. Punch a hole in the center by using a nail. Make a small hand like a clock with a hole in the wide end and laminate all the pieces. Cut the pieces apart and place a brad through the hand then through the 1/4 inch straw and last through the circle. This will be the spinner for the game.

To play the game, place the tree game board and the apple pieces on the table. Children will take turns spinning the spinner, saying the number and/or counting the dots. Then they will add that amount of apples to the tree. Continue the game until the all the apples are gone or the children lose interest.

This activity will help them recognize numerals and learn how many things the numeral represents. It also reinforces counting skills.

Pumpkin Game

Purchase small plastic pumpkins at a party store or dollar store that are open at the top and also small votive candles. You will need one set for each member of the small group and one for the teacher to demonstrate with. If not available use paper pumpkin shapes and birthday candles in place of the plastic pumpkins.

Use this game to teach position words – in, on, out, over, under, beside, in front of, and behind.

Instructions – Teacher will say one of the position words (like on the pumpkin) and place her candle on the pumpkin. Teacher will tell children to also place their candle on the pumpkin. Children will continue to place their candle in, behind or etc as teacher says the words and demonstrates. Teacher will take notice of the words children understand and which ones they need help doing. Continue play using most familiar word positions like in and on and adding less familiar ones as the children learn them. Use this activity more than one day, keeping it for short periods of time. When the children are beginning to understand where to put candles and the words used, have them take turns telling the other children where to put their candle and demonstrating where to put it.

Dot to Dot Bat Picture

Make a simple drawing of a bat and add dots at critical points. Next put a piece of thin piece of paper over the drawing and trace the dots only. Next put numeral 1-10 by the dots in the correct order needed to complete picture. Now copy the pattern as many times as you would like and laminate them. Provide a wipe off marker with the pictures and have the children complete the dot to dots starting with dot 1 and continuing in numeral order until the picture has been completed.

Spider Activity

Use the play dough recipe and color the dough. Divide the dough into small balls and place each one in a plastic ball with 8 pipe-cleaners. Pipe-cleaners should be cut into pieces about 2 inches long.

Children will learn about spiders while doing this activity. They will make a spider body by forming a small circle and large circle and joining them. Spiders have two parts to their body. Because spiders have eight legs, have the children stick eight small cut pipe-cleaners to form legs into the dough. They with count and use four legs on each side. Children will enjoy this counting activity and taking their spider's home. Include a small note with the spider and have parent ask child about the body number of parts and legs on a spider.

Goblin Grope

Use feely can (from Volume 1) or use a box with small hole for child's hand cut into it. Child puts hand through opening and feels a shape object and guesses the shape. Then child pulls object out and sees if the shape named was correct. Continue playing with same child or by taking turns with children in a small group. Objects could be apple to represent a circle, die for a square, domino for rectangle, wood block triangle for triangle, heart eraser for heart, plastic star tracer for star. You could also use food shapes for a gooey grope like grapes for ovals and cut square potato for squares.

Soft Play Dough

2 cups flour	Combine all ingredients in a medium sauce pan, mix well. Cook over low heat stirring constantly until mixture gathers and forms dough. Dump onto counter until cool enough to handle and then knead to form a ball. Store in a container or plastic bag.
1 cup salt	
2 cups water	
2 Tbs. cream of tartar	
2 Tbs. cooking oil	
*Food coloring optional	*Food coloring may be added to the water before mixing with the flour.

Play-dough Counting

Another activity for counting is used with cookie cutter shapes. You can use ghosts, pumpkins, witches, headstones, etc., and small rolling pins. Cut out and line up the shapes and count them. The next day they could also make a pattern with them. Start with two patterns and add up to four to expand their thinking skills when they can do smaller numbers of patters. This activity helps them see patterns in numerals and other things around them. This teaches them to solve problems.

FINE MOTOR SKILLS

Stencil Tracers

Use stencils of Halloween objects or make your own Halloween shapes with poster board and have children trace around them using colored pencils on a piece of while paper. Some shapes that you could make are pumpkins, bats, and ghosts. This develops writing skills.

Play Dough Pumpkins

Make soft orange play dough and have children make pumpkins of different sizes and shapes. You can also use the self hardening type. If using the self-hardening type you can leave it white or color it. Then when it dries out children can paint it with water colors or poster paint. This activity develops finger strength.

Self-Hardening Play Dough

4 cups flour
11/2 cups salt
1 tsp. alum

*Optional 1-2 Tbs. food coloring

Mix the flour, salt and alum together. Then add the water to it gradually.

*If you want mixture colored, add coloring to water before stirring into the flour for a smooth color.

Stir to form a ball in bowl. Add more water if it won't hold together. Next knead dough. Place in a sealed container until ready to use. After shapes have been made leave out to dry.

Pumpkin Paper Tearing Project

Teacher draws large pumpkin on a piece of white card-stock or construction paper. Children cut out the pumpkins. Then the teacher demonstrates how to tear colored paper into small pieces and glue them onto the pumpkin shape. They can use orange, yellow and green paper to create their pumpkin with a stem or they can make it into a jack-o-lantern with eyes, mouth and nose. You can also substitute other Halloween shapes such as a witch face, scarecrow, etc.

Bat Project

Use two paper plates to make a bat by having children cut on lines you make on them. Use lines like the ones below.

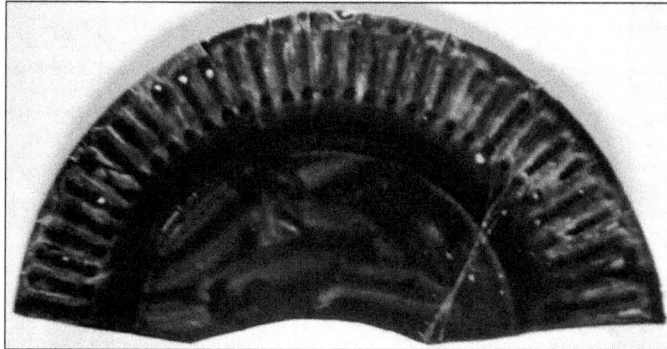

Then give each child two small square pieces of green construction paper and one rectangle piece of rectangle paper. Show children how to cut off corners on green square and smooth out to make two eyes. Next show them how to create a tongue from the red piece.

The next day have children paint their bat bodies and wings with black poster paint. While paint is wet, have the children add their two green eyes and a long red tongue. If it won't stick on to the wet paint then use some glue. When they are dry, hang them from the ceiling using fishing line and a thumbtack.

Simple Bat Project

Teacher provides bat pattern cut from poster board. Children can then trace bat shapes on to black construction paper with white chalk. Then children will cut their bat out. Next have craft eyes available to glue on to their bats. This activity helps develop cutting skills.

Spider web

Use a white paper plate then make a three inch long cuts around the edge every two to three inches. Cut a section of black yarn about thirty inches long and attach it to the back of the plate with tape. Children will weave yarn over and under and in and out of the slits on the edge of the plate. This will form a spider web. When that piece of yarn is used up, add another piece of yarn by taping it to the back of the plate. Then place a black spider ring through the yarn on the front side so that it shows the spider in its web. Continue weaving until all the yarn has been used up. Next the teacher tapes that end of yarn to back and the project is completed.

Simple Pumpkin

For a simple pumpkin use white paper plates and have children paint them with orange paint. Then have children glue on a simple green stem. When they are day hang them around the classroom. Or as an alternate idea, you can have children make them into jack-o-lanterns. Provide yellow construction paper squares, triangles and two different mouth shapes. Children will choose shapes of eyes, nose and mouth and glue them onto their pumpkins.

Simple Pictures

Teacher will show children how to draw several simple Halloween shapes like a ghost, bat, pumpkin or monster using colored chalk. Next children will be given black construction paper and told to use the colored chalk to create their own Halloween pictures.

Owl

Use an empty toilet paper roll for owl body. Squeeze top of roll together and staple it closed. Make brown paint or use tole paint and have children paint it brown. Use cardstock or poster board to make two small wings.

Cut wings out. Children will paint them with the body. When body and wings are dry, children will glue the wings on the owl body. They will also glue on two wiggly craft eyes and an orange beak made by you. To make beak use a small rectangle piece of orange construction paper. Fold it over and cut a narrow triangle shape with the wide base part forming the part they will attach to the owl for its beak.

LANGUAGE AND LITERACY

Pumpkin Game

Purchase small plastic pumpkins at a party store or dollar store that are open at the top and also small votive candles. You will need one set for each member of the small group and one for the teacher to demonstrate with. If not available use paper pumpkin shapes and birthday candles in place of the plastic pumpkins.

Use this game to teach position words – in, on, out, over, under, beside, in front of, and behind.

Instructions – Teacher will say one of the position words (like on the pumpkin) and place her candle on the pumpkin. Teacher will tell children to also place their candle on the pumpkin. Children will continue to place their candle in, behind or etc as teacher says the words and demonstrates. Teacher will take notice of the words children understand and which ones they need help doing. Continue play using most familiar word positions like in and on and adding less familiar ones as the children learn them. Use this activity more than one day, keeping it for short periods of time. When the children are beginning to understand where to put candles and the words used, have them take turns telling the other children where to put their candle and demonstrating where to put it.

Pretend Game

Use costumes for this activity. The costumes could be community helper or Halloween. Children in small group will take turns choosing a costume to put on. Next teacher will ask the children if the costumed child is a real (example-clown) or just pretending by wearing a clown costume. We will go through this activity until all the children in the small group have had a turn putting on a costume. Next as a class we will discuss more about what is real and what is pretend. This activity helps children to use expressive language and helps them learn the difference between real and pretend.

Finger Play Activity

Use a simple finger play such as <u>Five Little Pumpkins</u>. Repeat the words pointing to your fingers. You can also use pumpkin stickers on a ring of card stock for each finger to act it out or just put a sticker on each of the five fingers.

This activity will help children to increase their memory and learn sequence order.

Five Little Pumpkins

Five little pumpkins sitting on a gate,

The first one said, "Oh my, it's getting late." (point to 1st finger)

The second one said, "There are witches in the air".

The third one said, "But we don't care."

The fourth one said, "Let's run and run and run".

The fifth one said, "I'm ready for some fun."

"Oo-oo!" went the wind and out went the light, (clap your hands)

And the five little pumpkins rolled out of sight. (roll your hands)

Ghost Transition Activity

Sing this short chant. Let the children shout out the name and use their spookiest voice for the rest of the chant.

Ghost so scary,

Ghost so white,

Don't scare (child's name)! (Shout it out)

On Halloween night.

Halloween Game

Choose four small Halloween objects found at The Dollar Tree or Partyland, such as a plastic bat, a black cat, a small pumpkin and a small ghost. Use a piece of cloth or a hand towel. Show the items to the children. Say the names of each item while pointing to them. Tell the children that you are going to cover the items up and change their order. Children should study their order before the teacher covers them up. Next cover the items and change their positions. Uncover the items and start with the child to your left and have he/she put the items back in the order shown. If the children have a hard find doing this use only three items under they get better at doing it. Keep going to the left until all the children in the small group have had at least three turns. If they aren't tired of the game, have them take turns doing the teacher part. They move the items while they are covered and the other children put them back. When they are staring to get restless stop and continue another day. This activity helps children learn develop their visual memory.

Halloween Activity

Use pictures of ghosts, cats, bats, pumpkins etc. You will also need a black plastic cauldron and a large spoon. Show the pictures one at a time and have the children name each item. Then show two of more of the items and have them add the snake "s" sound. Discuss if teacher shows one bat we say bat, but if there is more than one bat we have to say bats. Then have the children take turns coming up to help make witches brew. Give each child one or more of the same pictures. They will say the item using plural "s" sound if more than one. Next they will as they add it to the caldron and stir with the spoon. The children will repeat the chant-stirring and stirring the witches brew. Put in the (say the name of the items - example bats) to make our brew. Children will learn vocabulary and how to say plural words.

FREE TIME

CREATIVE ARTS

Cut out large pumpkin shapes for the children to paint on. Clip the shapes to the easels. You can also have children cut out the pumpkin shapes days before using the paint or on the same day that the paint is out. Mix orange, yellow and green poster paints in containers to be used with paint brushes or use sponge painting on the pumpkins.

Children will dip the sponge into the paint and then press it on to the pumpkin shape. To make the sponges cut regular household sponges into squares, triangles, and circles. Next mount the sponges onto blocks of wood or empty spools of thread by gluing them onto the top or bottom. This will help the children keep their fingers clean while painting.

Use shallow containers in the tray with poster paint left thick and only a half of inch or so deep. Don't forget to mix the paint with a little dish detergent to help the paint come out of children's clothes easier.

Children can create their own pumpkin or make them into a jack-o-lantern. Other fall shapes can be used on the easel for different days such as large leaf shapes and different squash shapes. You could make a picture of a house and have the children "haunt" it with the paint as well.

SENSORY

Place a large pumpkin or squash inside the table. Have the pumpkin or squash cut open so children can explore the insides using spoons.

Use a collection of fall leaves mixed with pinecones to explore. Add hidden small shapes later for the children to find. Add plastic spiders or other bugs.

Make green goblin goop and children to play in and see how a solid changes to a liquid in their hands.

Green Goblin Goop

Use 1 part water to 2 parts corn starch and add enough green washable poster paint to make color desired. Mix together the liquids with the corn starch. The mixture will look like a solid, but when you take a handful, it will become runny and drip out of your hand. If the mixture is too runny and will not form a solid ball add more corn starch. If the mixture is too hard, add a little more water.

DRAMATIC PLAY & SOCIAL DEVELOPMENT

Have a box of costumes or community helper clothing for children to wear. You could also use a box of Halloween costumes. A good place to find these items would be at a local Thrift Store.

SCIENCE

Make witches brew by adding dry ice to any juice. Be sure and use a large container. Put juice into container and add dry ice to it and watch the steaming results. Never touch the dry ice with your hands. Use tongs or special thick dry gloves. After the steaming shows down, use a ladle to pour into cups to serve it. It will now be carbonated like soda pop. Talk about the gas that was created by the dry ice. You could ask children what might happen if you put the dry ice into other liquids and then try a few out.

GROSS MOTOR SKILLS

Pumpkin Pitch

Pitch bean bags into a large pumpkin mouth. Make it by using an orange poster and attaching it to the front of a large open box.

Spooky Walk

Use the tape from list called Spooky Walk and have the children pretend to take a spooky walk while acting out the song.

Witches Walk

Use the tape Witches Brew from list to play while the children walk around the circle. The circle will have varies Halloween shapes taped to the floor but there should be less pictures than children. Tell them that when the music stops, they should see if they landed on a shape. When they land on a shape reward them with a small prize such as a Halloween right and sit down. Continue playing until all children have won a prize and are sitting down.

Witch Swat

Use Mylar balloons with Halloween pictures on them, but only have air in them. They should not float. Place children in small groups with room to move. Tell them to try and keep the witches or other Halloween picture balloons up in the air and not land on the floor. Tell them to have fun and help each other keep them up, but use care not to hit other children.

Pumpkin Hop

Place pictures of pumpkins on the floor in a circle or other shape. Children will hop from one pumpkin to another when music starts or teacher says go and stop when music stops and she says freeze. Teacher will tell them different movement the next time like tip toe and stomp. Continue for two or three times and then stop until another day. If you stop playing before they are tired of it they will want to play again another day.

FIELD TRIP IDEAS

Pumpkin Patch

Arrange to have the children visit a pumpkin patch to see how they grow. If possible also make arrangements for the children to pick their own pumpkin from a group of modestly priced ones. The children can paint them in class another day to take home.

Bats & Spiders

🎵 MUSIC AND MOVEMENT

Sing the following songs with your class:

"There's A Spider on the Floor" found on CD Raffi *Singsable Songs for the Very Young*

"The Itsy Bitsy Spider" found on tape *Barney's Favorites*

"I know an Old Lady" found in *Sing-along & Fingerplays* by Susan Finkel and Karen Seberg

"Spooky Walk" by John Given found in Macmillan *Sing and Learn*

📝 LANGUAGE AND LITERACY

The following are a list of great spider and bat books. Because there are so many, choose your favorites and read multiple books throughout the unit.

The Eensy-Weensy Spider adapted by Mary Ann Hoberman

Zipping, Zapping, Zooming Bats by Ann Earle

Bat Jamboree by Kathi Appelt

Stellaluna by Janell Cannon

Bat Child's Haunted House by Mercer Mayer

Spider on The Floor illustrated by True Kelly

The Very Busy Spider by Eric Carle

Stellaluna is a great book with beautiful pictures to teach important social skill. It shows how being different is not necessarily bad and how to get along with others can help you.

SMALL GROUP ACTIVITIES/TABLE TIMES

MATH AND COGNITIVE

Dot to Dot Bat Picture

Make a simple drawing of a bat and add dots at critical points. Next put a piece of thin piece of paper over the drawing and trace the dots only. Next put numeral 1-10 by the dots in the correct order needed to complete picture. Now copy the pattern as many times as you would like and laminate them. Provide a wipe off marker with the pictures and have the children complete the dot to dots starting with dot 1 and continuing in numeral order until the picture has been completed.

Spider Activity

Use the play dough receipt and color the dough. Divide the dough into small balls and place each one in a plastic ball with 8 pipe-cleaners. Pipe-cleaners should be cut into pieces about 2 inches long. Children will learn about spiders while doing this activity. They will make a spider body by forming a small circle and large circle and joining them. Spiders have two parts to their body. Next spiders have eight legs, so children will stick eight small cut pipe-cleaners to form legs into the dough. They with count and use four legs on each side. Children will enjoy this counting activity and taking their spider's home. Include a small note with the spider and have parent ask child about the body number of parts and legs on a spider.

Make a Spider

Provide cut up egg cartons that are cut into individual egg sections. Cut four small holes on each side for the legs. Give each child pipe cleaners to make the spider legs. Use craft eyes or let the children decorate the entire body and face.

Goblin Grope

Use feely can (from book 1), or use box with small hole for child's hand cut into it. Child puts hand through opening and feels a shape object and guesses the shape. Then child pulls object out and sees if the shape named was correct. Continue playing with same child or by taking turns with children in a small group. Objects could be apple for a circle, die for a square, domino for rectangle, wood block triangle for triangle, heart eraser for heart, plastic star tracer for star. You could also use food shapes for a gooey grope like grapes for ovals and cut square potato for squares.

Soft Play Dough

2 cups flour
1 cup salt
2 cups water
2 Tbs. cream of tartar
2 Tbs. cooking oil

*Food coloring optional

Combine all ingredients in a medium sauce pan, mix well. Cook over low heat stirring constantly until mixture gathers and forms a dough. Dump onto counter until cool enough to handle and then knead to form a ball. Store in a container or plastic bag.

*Food coloring may be added to the water before mixing with the flour.

FINE MOTOR SKILLS

Stencil Tracers

Use stencils of bats and spiders or make your own with poster board and have children trace around them using colored pencils on a piece of while paper. This helps develop writing skills.

Bat Project

Use two paper plates to make a bat by having children cut on lines you make on them. Use lines like the ones below.

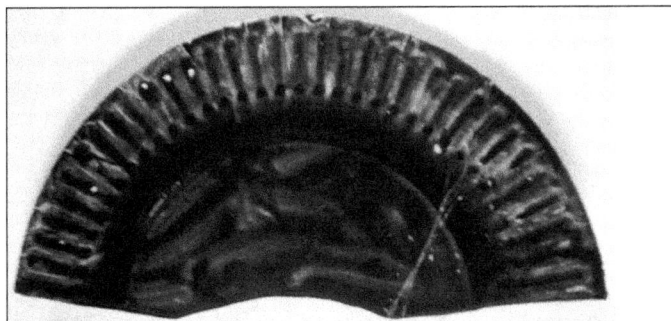

Then give each child two small square pieces of green construction paper and one rectangle piece of rectangle paper. Show children how to cut off corners on green square and smooth out to make two eyes. Next show them how to create a tongue from the red piece. The next day have children paint their bat bodies and wings with black poster paint. While paint is wet, have them add their two green eyes and a long red tongue. If it won't stick on to the wet paint use some glue. When they are dry, hang them from the ceiling using fishing line with a thumbtack.

Simple Bat Project

Teacher provides bat pattern cut from poster board. Children trace bat shapes on to black construction paper with white chalk. Then children will cut their bat out. Next have craft eyes available to glue on to their bats. This activity helps develop cutting skills.

Spider Web

Get a white paper plate and make cuts around edge every two to three inches. The cuts should be about three inches long. Cut a piece of black yarn about thirty inches long and attach it to the back of the plate with tape. Children will weave yarn over and under and in and out of the slits on the edge of the plate. This will form a spider web. When that piece of yarn is used up, add another piece of yarn by taping it to the back of the plate. Then place a black spider ring through the yarn on the front side to that it shows the spider in its web. Continue weaving until all the yarn has been used up. Next the teacher tapes that end of yarn to back and the project is completed.

LANGUAGE AND LITERACY

The children will enjoy this finger play about bats.

Five Little Bats

1 little bat was trying to behave.

He hung upside down from his feet in a cave.

Another bat flew in, and said, "How do you do?"

The second joined the first, and then there were 2!

2 little bats were trying to behave.

They hung upside down from their feet in a cave.

To help pass the time, they sang "Do re me"

Another bat joined the song, and then there were 3.

3 little bats were trying to behave

They hung upside down from their feet in a cave

From their cave perch, they looked down at the floor,

A new bat joined the game, and then there were 4.

4 little bats were trying to behave.

They hung upside down from their feet in a cave.

One little bat zoomed inside and did a dive.

He stayed to take a rest, and with him there were 5.

Also sing this song set to the tune of **"Ten Little Indians"**:

Spin, spin, little spider,

Spin, spin, wider, wider.

Spin, spin, little spider,

Early in the morning.

Dance, dance, little spider,

Dance, Dance, Dance out wider.

Dance, dance, little spider,

Early in the morning.

Sing again but change action verbs to "jump, crawl, run, etc."

FREE TIME

CREATIVE ARTS

Cut out large bat or spider shapes for the children to paint on. Clip the shapes to the easels. You can also have children cut out the shapes days before using the paint or on the same day that the paint is out. Mix poster paints in containers to be used with paint brushes or use sponge painting on the pictures.

Children will dip the sponge into the paint and then press it on to the shape. To make the sponges cut regular household sponges into squares, triangles, and circles. Next mount the sponges onto blocks of wood or empty spools of thread by gluing them onto the top or bottom. This will help the children keep their fingers clean while painting.

Use shallow containers in the tray with poster paint left thick and only a half of inch or so deep. Don't forget to mix the paint with a little dish detergent to help the paint come out of children's clothes easier.

SENSORY

Purchase some large plastic spiders. Put these at the sensory table so children can see what all the small parts look like. You may also want to include real spiders that have been preserved in plastic blocks so you can observe them up close. Include a magnifying glass.

DRAMATIC PLAY & SOCIAL DEVELOPMENT

Have a box of costumes or community helper clothing for children to wear. You could also use a box of Halloween costumes. A good place to find these items would be at a local Thrift Store.

SCIENCE

Display a collection of spiders that have been killed in a jar and then pined to a display board. It is best if they are inside a glass or plastic covered box to protect the collection. You can collect your own or check out local colleges for the loan out collections. Place books about spiders on the table too.

Place a pail and add some plastic spiders and other creepy crawly things like rubber bats and snakes. Don't forget to include books here with lots of pictures and information about the items in the pail.

GROSS MOTOR SKILLS

Spooky Walk

Use the tape from list called Spooky Walk and have the children pretend to take a spooky walk while acting out the song.

Bat Swat

Use Mylar balloons with spiders and bat pictures on them, but only have air in them. They should not float. Place children in small groups with room to move. Tell them to try and keep the spiders and bat balloons up in the air and not land on the floor. Tell them to have fun and help each other keep them up, but use care not to hit other children.

Spider Hop

Place pictures of bats or spiders on the floor in a circle. Children will hop from one pumpkin to another when music starts or teacher says go and stop when music stops and she says freeze. Teacher will tell them different movement the next time like tip toe and stomp. Continue for 2 or 3 times and then stop until another day. If you stop playing before they are tired of it they will want to play again another day.

FIELD TRIP IDEAS

Visit a local cave where children can see bats, spiders or just the area in which they would like to live. Generally operated by state or government officials, these caves offer a unique opportunity to show children different types of bats.

Another field trip can be taken to a pet store where they have tarantulas on display. Many times the staff will handle or let the children handle these spiders.

Go to a local park or wooded area to find and capture your own spider specimens. Make sure that you are educated on any possible poisonous spiders in your area and/or modify this activity by finding them in advance and putting them in an observation tank, glass or box for the children to watch.

Where To Get What You Need

There are many different places to get what you need. If you use your imagination, many items can be substituted for what you have on hand, can get for free, etc. For example, you may have an abundance of baby food jars from a family toddler. You can easily convert these to be part of a project. Teaching is also about being resourceful. Have family, friends, students and yourself save:

- Baby food jars

- Toilet paper rolls

- Paper towel rolls

- Scraps of material

- Extra tile

- Extra pieces from home improvement projects

- Coffee cans

- Oatmeal containers

- 2 liter bottles

- Cereal boxes

- Egg carton

- Milk jugs

- Salt containers

- Anything you can think of to be re-purposed for a learning tool

Other places to get materials include:

- Home improvement stores (Lowes or Home Depot)

- Dollar Stores

- Educational Supply Stores

- Grocery Store

- Party Supply Store

- Online Resources:

  — Oriental Trading Company: www.orientaltrading.com

  — http://www.etacuisenaire.com